C000192690

Change Your Life
IN 5 MINUTES A DAY

Inspiring Ideas to Vitalize Your Life

JOANNE MALLON

CHANGE YOUR LIFE IN 5 MINUTES A DAY

Copyright © Summersdale Publishers Ltd, 2021

All rights reserved.

No part of this book may be reproduced by any means, nor transmitted, nor translated into a machine language, without the written permission of the publishers.

Joanne Mallon has asserted her moral right to be identified as the author of this work in accordance with sections 77 and 78 of the Copyright, Designs and Patents Act 1988.

Condition of Sale
This book is sold subject to the condition that it shall not, by way of trade or otherwise, be lent, resold, hired out or otherwise circulated in any form of binding or cover other than that in which it is published and without a similar condition including this condition being imposed on the subsequent purchaser.

An Hachette UK Company
www.hachette.co.uk

Vie Books, an imprint of Summersdale Publishers Ltd
Part of Octopus Publishing Group Limited
Carmelite House
50 Victoria Embankment
LONDON
EC4Y 0DZ
UK

www.summersdale.com

Printed and bound in the Czech Republic

ISBN: 978-1-78783-636-5

Substantial discounts on bulk quantities of Summersdale books are available to corporations, professional associations and other organizations. For details contact general enquiries: telephone: +44 (0) 1243 771107 or email: enquiries@summersdale.com.

Contents

Introduction

Our lives pivot on tiny moments. Whether it's an email out of the blue, someone saying yes to you, someone saying no, births, deaths, accidents or decisions, these instants form turning points in our lives and all of a sudden we're headed in a new direction. This book contains over 60 ideas to make that new direction a choice rather than a reaction, and all of them take just 5 minutes to do.

These tips are structured across the day, though you can do them whenever fits in best with your schedule. Most of them don't need extra resources but some may require a journal for you to write in — if you don't have one, any scrap of paper or the notes app on your phone will do. Try picking just one to start with: the tip that seems easiest or speaks to you the loudest. Once that's embedded in your life, add on any others that appeal. These ingredients will transform your life and give you a fresh perspective on your daily routine.

AM I GOOD ENOUGH?
YES I AM.

MICHELLE OBAMA

Chapter One

Morning Miracles

Every day is a fresh page. Start your day on a positive note and you're already moving upwards! Mornings are when motivation and energy levels are highest, making new, positive habits easier to begin.

Behavioural science tells us that it's easiest to add a new habit on to an existing one, so try slotting the following tips into your current daily rhythms; perhaps after brushing your teeth or on your daily commute. Read through this section the night before and plan which tip you're going to take up. Placing a notebook and pen by the bed might also help to remind you in the morning.

Set your intentions

Think about what's in your diary for today. What's the most important task on your to-do list? Get pinpoint specific on what you intend to do and when you'll do it. If there's something that might stop that from happening, how will you deal with it? When you decide on an action point, write it down. Make an appointment in your calendar and set a reminder if you think you'll forget. Obstacles become easier to handle and you will feel more confident once you have a plan.

You are the only one who
gets to decide what you will
be remembered for.

Taylor Swift

BREATHE IN CONFIDENCE

This is a trick used by professional speakers to help them feel calm and confident. Place your dominant hand on your stomach, on the area that goes in and out most noticeably when you breathe. Take relaxed, full breaths, feeling the abdomen pull in then out again. Deep breathing like this slows the heart rate, making you feel centred and ready to face the world. Practise this a few times when you're already feeling calm, so you'll know how to do it anytime you need to reconnect with your most confident self.

TAKE A STRETCH

You can do this one without even
leaving your bed! Pull your arms up and
out above your head and extend your legs
with your toes pointed as far as they can go. Relax,
and then stretch again, even further this time
if you can. Take a moment to thank your
body for everywhere it has carried you
throughout your life and all the
places it will carry you to today.

DANCE TO THE MUSIC

When you're dressed for the day and about to get going, play your favourite feel-good tune and lose yourself in 5 minutes of dance. Which band did you love when you were younger? Who haven't you listened to in a long time? What song always makes you turn up the volume when you hear it on the radio? Put your phone down, crank up the music and dance. It's guaranteed to put a smile on your face.

Turn off and tune in

Before you launch yourself into a busy day, go through your phone settings and turn off as many app notifications as you can. Notifications interrupt the flow of your day and suck up your attention by dragging you back into the online world. If you're cutting down on screen activity, wearing a watch will also help by stopping you picking up your phone to check the time.

YOU ARE
PERFECTLY
CAST IN YOUR
LIFE. I CAN'T
IMAGINE
ANYONE
BUT YOU IN
THE ROLE.
GO PLAY.

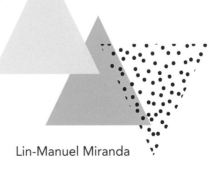

Lin-Manuel Miranda

Visualize the day you want

Sit quietly and think about your day ahead. Think your way through each hour from morning to evening, about the conversations you will have. How do you want to walk through this day? What would you like to have achieved by the end of it? Make a list if it helps you to visualize things. Then, when you meet your daily challenges, your brain is better prepared to help you cope.

Set an alarm for anything you definitely want to happen. Instead of relying on yourself to remember all your tasks, be it phoning your family, fitting in some yoga, or submitting that report in the morning, set a reminder on your phone so that it definitely happens. This will stop the day from running away with you without anything getting done. Setting an alarm is particularly useful if you're trying to take up a brand new habit, because it will take a few weeks for it to become an automatic behaviour.

IF YOU TRULY POUR YOUR HEART INTO WHAT YOU BELIEVE IN, EVEN IF IT MAKES YOU VULNERABLE, AMAZING THINGS CAN AND WILL HAPPEN.

EMMA WATSON

Find a new path

Shaking up your usual morning routine by doing something out of the ordinary is a great way to fire up your creativity. Today, why not take a new route to work? Drive down a different road, or walk along a street you've never been to before. You could even switch to running or cycling if you usually walk. And if you work from home, invent your own commute with a short walk outside to start your day. Small changes like this that take you out of your comfortable routine can be the catalyst for bigger changes in your life.

Mindfulness meditation

A short meditation session will quickly help you relax, de-stress and become more productive. Moreover, it will teach you to be more aware of what's going on in your body and mind. You can set a timer for this or just trust yourself to know when you feel ready to stop. A longer stretch of meditation for up to 20 minutes will bring even more benefits, but 5 minutes is a good place to start. Start with one or two sessions a week, gradually turning this into a daily habit (or more frequently if you feel it's beneficial to you).

Sit or lie down in a quiet, comfortable space. Close your eyes and inhale for a count of five. Feel the breath as it travels slowly through your body. Gently hold the breath, then exhale for another count of five. As you exhale, picture any stress or tension leaving your body, melting away into nothingness or dripping like rainwater from the tips of your fingers. Keep your focus on your body and what you can feel. If you get distracted by thoughts, set them aside for later or watch them drift past like clouds in the sky.

SING A SONG

Why does belting out a tune in the shower feel so good? Singing is a natural antidepressant and an underrated stress reducer – it releases endorphins, the feel-good brain chemical, plus the deep breathing you need to sing draws more oxygen into the blood and improves circulation. Have fun and get your show tune on as you prepare for the day.

TOMORROW IS A NEW DAY, WITH NO MISTAKES IN IT YET.

L. M. MONTGOMERY

Amp up your senses

The first time you step outside your door today, take a few minutes to focus on what you can see, hear, smell, taste and touch. Listen to the birds in the trees and the people's voices around you. What can you hear in the distance? How is the air different today? What has changed since yesterday? Take a few moments to engage with every sense, becoming still and present in your body. This will help you build a calm mental platform from which to deal with your busy day.

5
MINUTES
OF SILENCE

This isn't as structured as
meditation; it's just a time for you to
tune in with whatever's buzzing around
in your mind. Leave your phone in another
room if you know you have a tendency to check it.
Turn off the TV, radio or anything else you can hear.
Simply sit and be with your thoughts, enjoying
the peaceful quiet and solitude. If your
household is busy then you may need
to retreat to the quietest room,
but at least a 5-minute
bathroom break is
easy to fit into
your day.

Use the good body lotion

What could you add to your morning routine to make it more of a pleasure? What have you been saving for best that you could use to treat yourself with today? The aim here is to spend 5 minutes being physically kind to yourself. It doesn't have to be body lotion – it could be your more expensive perfume or aftershave, or the fancy shower gel you got for Christmas but haven't opened yet. Treat yourself with kindness and generosity – today is all the special occasion you need.

Make friends with your body and appreciate it for its perfection. It is worth taking care of. You are worth taking care of. Using your special products is a small way of saying thank you to your body, by treating it as the precious and unique wonder it is. It's important to recognize your skin and limbs for all they do for you – they have carried you through so far and will support you today. No more saving things for best – your best starts now.

I AM NOT WHAT HAPPENED TO ME. I AM WHAT I CHOOSE TO BECOME.

CARL JUNG

CREATE A POSITIVE MANTRA

Mantras are positive phrases that we repeat out loud to help us feel calmer. They can be a great rudder to hold on to when your life is going off course, and you can use them to steer yourself back to centre. Your mantra could be as simple as "Be Calm", "All Is Well" or "Stay Strong". Check out the motivational quotes in this book – maybe one of them could be a new positive flag for you. Write one out and stick it where you'll see it often.

Be childish

Congratulations, you have won 5 silly minutes to let yourself go! Have a tantrum; punch a cushion; do a silly dance or sing a funny song. Before you get caught up in the stresses of the adult world, allow yourself to live in the moment just like children do. People of all ages learn better when they play, so allow yourself some time for fun. Don't worry about the future or overthink problems of the past. Let yourself go freely into the flow of just being rather than having to be on top of things all the time.

YOU ARE NOT THE WORK YOU DO; YOU ARE THE PERSON YOU ARE.

Toni Morrison

Three-ingredient energy bars

Whip up a batch of these no-bake, easy energy bars and you'll be armed with healthy snacks for the next few days. All you need are dates, plus any combination of dried fruit and nuts that you enjoy. This recipe makes 10 to 20 bars depending on size and shape.

Ingredients:

1 cup of dates (make sure the stones are removed)

1 cup of nuts (almonds, walnuts, pistachios or cashews all work well)

1 cup of dried fruit (e.g. dried cherries, apricots or cranberries)

1 handful of seeds of your choice, or dried coconut (optional)

Method:

Use any teacup or coffee mug to measure, so long as it's the same for all three ingredients.

Add all the ingredients to the bowl of a food processor (throw in a handful of seeds or dried coconut if you like), and pulse until you get a smooth mixture.

Line a baking tin with foil or baking paper, then press the mixture into the tin.

Cut into bars; or shape it into balls if you prefer – the mixture should be firm enough to do so.

Chill in the refrigerator for a few hours to firm up. Keeps in the fridge for up to a fortnight.

GO CONFIDENTLY IN THE DIRECTION OF YOUR DREAMS! LIVE THE LIFE YOU'VE IMAGINED.

HENRY DAVID THOREAU

Write a postcard

Remember when we used to send postcards from holiday rather than post Facebook updates? Postcards are a wonderful way to share happy times with your favourite people. Why not scribble a quick message to someone to let them know that you're thinking of them? A handwritten message is a unique and very personal snapshot of what you're thinking now and a thoughtful way to connect with a loved one. No need to wait until your next holiday!

Drink a cup of green tea

Packed with antioxidants and polyphenols, green tea has been credited with everything including improving brain function, lowering the risk of some cancers, boosting metabolic rate, improving blood flow and lowering cholesterol. Who wouldn't want a cup of that? If you don't like the taste, there are many flavoured green teas available that will still give you the benefits and have you starting your day with a bang!

CELEBRATE YOURSELF

Write down three things that you like about yourself. If you're struggling, you'll find some clues in what other people admire about you. What do they come to you for? What do your partner or friends say are your good points? What are you proud of? Turning the spotlight on yourself can be a surprisingly challenging thing to do, but it's important to appreciate yourself. Keep this list where you can refer to it easily, and add to it when you think of something new. Be your own cheerleader as you value all that you contribute to the world.

Chapter Two

Make My Day!

Whether you spend the majority of your time in an office, a classroom or at home, there are plenty of ways to transform the everyday into something more spectacular. By looking for little opportunities to brighten your day, you'll cast a better light on the whole picture. Focus on what you definitely will do today, not the things you feel you should do. Trying is not the same as doing and "shoulds" are other people's goals. Instead ask yourself: What do I need? What do I want? What will I do? When will I start?

Take a small action where it matters

As you start your working day, take a moment to identify your most important upcoming task, then work on it for 5 minutes. It might be something you find difficult or have been putting off for a while, but just giving it a tiny amount of attention will help get the ball rolling. Sometimes not doing something is more draining than the energy it would take to make a start on that challenge. Just 5 minutes' worth, then you can move on to something else, but chances are that's all you need for the next step to naturally occur.

Start where you are. Use what you have. Do what you can.

Arthur Ashe

The 5-4-3-2-1

This mindfulness exercise is widely used and recommended by psychologists and experts in the field of anxiety. It's a way of moving focus from your mind to your body – the five senses in particular.

Start by identifying 5 things you can see. Then, list 4 things you can hear; 3 things you can feel; 2 things you can smell and 1 thing you can taste. This will bring your attention to the present and what is, rather than allowing your mind to spin off into what ifs. In the process, anxious feelings are pushed firmly into the background – they may even disappear altogether!

Keep this exercise in your toolkit to use any time you're feeling anxious or starting to panic. Practise it a few times even when you're feeling fine, so you'll know what to do when you need it.

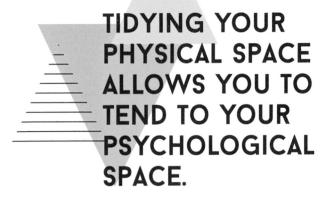

TIDYING YOUR PHYSICAL SPACE ALLOWS YOU TO TEND TO YOUR PSYCHOLOGICAL SPACE.

Marie Kondo

TAKE FIVE THINGS OUT OF YOUR WARDROBE

Streamlining your wardrobe will help you appreciate the clothes you choose to keep. A full wardrobe declutter may be too much to manage all at once, but you can lose five things easily, right? You probably won't even notice that they're gone. What haven't you worn for a year? What doesn't fit? Take five things you don't wear out of your wardrobe and put them in a bag, ready for the charity shop. You'll feel great knowing you've given your clothes a second life.

SIT DOWN AND WATCH THE BIRDS

As you go through your day, look out
for animals – they've got lots to teach us.
Sitting quietly and watching birds will help you
get closer to nature. You'll develop better patience
and attention to detail whilst becoming calmer
and more relaxed. Watch for long enough
and it becomes almost meditative.
What do you notice in the way they
interact with each other? How
can you apply that to your
interactions with the
people you meet
today?

THESE THINGS WILL BE HARD TO DO, BUT YOU CAN DO HARD THINGS.

GLENNON DOYLE

Learn a new word

Learning new words will give your memory a boost by challenging it to create more ways of retaining information. Not only will it expand your vocabulary, but it's also been known to improve cognitive ability. There are lots of apps that will give you a new word every day – or a word in a foreign language if you really want to stretch your brain. Saying your new words out loud will help you memorize them. Think about how you can throw this word into conversation – even if it's only to say, "Hey, I learned a new word today."

5-minute vent

Don't carry your anger with you throughout the day. Instead, decant your frustration into your journal, or the air, or the ear of a loved one. The aim here is to download those negative feelings out of your brain and leave space for something more productive. Give yourself 5 minutes to process the emotion, then get rid of it and consider what you can learn from it.

Think yourself confident

This is a method life coaches often use to help clients focus on what it might take to move from the life you have to the life you want. You can be your own life coach simply by asking yourself – if I was operating at 100 per cent confidence, what would I be doing differently? What would be happening in my life that isn't happening now? Surprisingly, the difference may not be as much as you might assume.

Once you've got a clear picture of where you want to be, start thinking about the best way to get there. You don't need to know the full path – just the first step. For example, if you wanted to change your job, consider updating your resume. Write down this first step in as much detail as possible. When will you do it? What do you need to make it happen? How will you know when it's done? Who do you need to tell so you won't back out? Take the first step and the momentum you create will ensure that the step after that follows easily.

A dream is only a dream...
until you decide to make it real.

Harry Styles

PLAN
YOUR
CAFFEINE
CUT-OFF POINT

Whilst everyone's sensitivity to
caffeine is different, many people find
that it interferes with sleep and can increase
anxiety. Make your caffeine consumption mindful
rather than automatic. Plan your caffeine cut-off
point today – for many people around
3 p.m. works best to prevent interfering
with sleep. There are a multitude of
delicious caffeine-free drinks
available. Why not spend
the next few afternoons
sampling some
new options?

GO OUTSIDE AND LOOK FOR SOMETHING BEAUTIFUL

If you're working indoors all day, shake up your day by taking 5 minutes to go outside. Look around until you find something beautiful, then take a photo and share it with your friends. If you look for something beautiful then you will find it, and by using it to connect with your community you are deepening those relationships too.

IF YOU DON'T LIKE THE ROAD YOU'RE WALKING, START PAVING ANOTHER ONE.

DOLLY PARTON

5-minute HIIT workout

HIIT stands for High Intensity Interval Training, and involves a short burst of action followed by a short recovery period. As well as lowering blood pressure, reducing body fat and improving cardiovascular health, high-intensity training also offers an array of mental health benefits, reducing levels of stress, anxiety and depression.

If you'd like to exercise more but you don't have time to go to the gym, this quick HIIT workout can be done anywhere in your home, or even on a break at work. You don't need much space or any special equipment and it'll fit easily into a small gap in your day.

30 seconds of ski jumps

30 seconds of high knee run

30 seconds of jumping jacks

30 seconds of recovery

Do as many rounds as you can until 5 minutes have elapsed.

For a more advanced workout, increase the activity to 40 seconds and decrease the recovery to 20 seconds.

I am capable of what every
other human is capable of.
This is one of the great
lessons of war and life.

Maya Angelou

Random acts of kindness

By giving something of yourself to others without any expectation of return, you'll increase your own feelings of self-worth. Studies have even shown that people who are kinder have 23 per cent less cortisol (the stress hormone) and age slower than the average population. Doing something kind for another person is like igniting a smile within yourself. Hold the door open for a stranger; pick up litter; give a gift. Large or small acts of kindness benefit everyone including you and can bring a big return for a small amount of effort.

Upskill

What's one skill you think would benefit your work? How are things changing in your industry and what do you need to know to keep up? Developing a skill could help you take the next step forward in your career, or even just make you feel more confident in your current position. Spend 5 minutes reading an article about whatever that skill is, and maybe even book yourself onto a training course.

EATING FOR SELF-CARE

When it comes to lunchtime, don't just grab the nearest thing. Take a moment to connect with your body and ask what it needs for nourishment today. Pause before you make or buy your lunch and think about what you need, rather than what you think you might want, or feel you "should" have. What will help you feel satisfied and fuel you across the rest of the day?

◆ ◆ ◆ ◆ ◆ ◆ ◆ ◆ ◆ ◆ ◆ ◆ ◆ ◆ ◆

Print out a photo

How many times have you told yourself you'll do this? A happy photo can light up a room, but too often we leave them hidden on the devices they were taken with. Today's the day you're going to display them proudly in your home! Choose your favourite photo of a loved one from your phone or camera and print it out. If you don't have a printer at home then many high street shops can help, or there are a number of apps that will do this directly from your device.

**FALL DOWN
SEVEN TIMES,
STAND UP
EIGHT.**

Japanese proverb

Plant a seed

Every day we sow seeds for our future lives without really realizing it, so do it today with purpose. Plant something in your garden now that will give you future joy when you least expect it.

You don't necessarily need a big area for a 5-minute gardening project – cress seeds on a window ledge work well, or you could simply pull a few weeds to tidy up your outdoor space. Dig deep into the soil and get your hands dirty. If you have more time on your hands, plant a flower that will give you pleasure when it blooms – fresh daffodils or tulips are particularly beautiful in springtime – or some fresh herbs to use in your next recipe. A crown of rhubarb will grow very well in a small space with the added benefit of being delicious in a number of desserts.

There's no pressure here to overhaul the whole garden, just take a few minutes to enjoy connecting with the growing world as you create a little corner of joy.

MAKE A BIRTHDAY BUCKET LIST

Make a list of all the things you'd like to achieve by the time your next landmark birthday rolls around. Get clear on what you want – the clearer you are on what you're aiming for, the more likely you are to hit that goal. How far are you from those things now? Pick the easiest one and make a start, aiming to complete one thing every few months until the big day.

Drink a glass of water

Staying hydrated throughout the day helps your body function in many ways, from supporting your joints, to keeping your kidneys healthy, to improving concentration and curing constipation. To make this habit stick, add it on to something you already do frequently, like checking your social media or going into the kitchen for a hot drink. If it helps, you can use an app to track your daily water consumption.

Chapter Three

Exceptional Evenings

It's the end of the day – time to wind down, reflect, take stock of the day that's gone and make plans for the days to come. Take this opportunity to nourish yourself both mentally and physically. Don't be too hard on yourself if you didn't achieve what you intended to today – another fresh page is on its way. There will be nuggets of gold in today and if you look, you will find them. The following tips will help you get the best out of your evening as you wind down and enjoy a restful night's sleep.

Get the gratitude habit

Start a gratitude journal by noting three things you're thankful for today. There is no rule as to how big or small they can be, and over time you'll notice how your outlook changes. By training yourself to look for the good in your life you will naturally start to appreciate what you have rather than long for the things you feel you lack. As your focus becomes more positive, so will other aspects of your life.

DAY BY DAY, WHAT YOU CHOOSE, WHAT YOU THINK AND WHAT YOU DO IS WHO YOU BECOME.

ANONYMOUS

Make a To-Don't list

Writing a list can be incredibly helpful when it comes to focusing your thoughts on the things you want to do. But what about the things you don't want? How clear are you on those? Do you ever find yourself agreeing to plans when you later wish you'd said no? Time to get out that paper and pen again.

Make a list of ten things you're not going to do tomorrow, this week, or ever. It could be things you've said yes to in the past but want to say no to in the future. It could be relationships or commitments that you need to move on from because they're not supporting you. This is your To-Don't list, the opposite of your to-do list. Getting clear on what your priorities are now will help you know if they are challenged in the future.

How you take care of yourself is how the world sees you. It's OK to have a relationship with yourself.

Jonathan Van Ness

GIVE YOUR BRAIN A REST

Doing something easy and repetitive gives your brain a rest and helps you to process everything that's happened throughout the day. Try crocheting or knitting a few lines, folding your laundry or dusting the nearest bookcase. Activities that involve repetition are good for managing anxiety, since they help the mind to balance. When your brain is forced to concentrate on physical movements, it's shifted into a state of flow and will release the worries it has been hanging on to. Ideal for winding down at the end of the day!

CHANGE YOUR CHARGING STATION

This is a one-time habit that could make a big difference to the whole of your life! Many studies show that using your phone just before bed can interfere with sleep quality. To combat this, decide on a new location for your device's charger, away from your bedroom, and make that its new home during your bedtime. It might be a tough habit to break at first, but your mind and body will thank you in the long run.

IT'S YOUR VOICE. CHERISH IT. RESPECT IT. NURTURE IT. CHALLENGE IT.

Dave Grohl

Colour me calm

As well as being a fun and creative activity, colouring is a wonderful way to unwind. The repetitive action takes your brain into a meditative state which helps relieve stress and reduce anxiety. It can even help you get a better night's sleep, as it provides a screen-free way to relax. Keep a colouring book and some pencils easily to hand and work it into your daily schedule – perhaps when you sit down after your evening meal – and let your creativity flow!

Lock in the learning

Write down one thing you learned today. This could be something small, such as a fun fact learned from a colleague, or something much bigger about yourself. Even a bad day can teach you what not to do, or how to do something differently next time. Being mindful of these little daily lessons allows you to be more open to change and growth. What will you take from today that's useful to you?

Watch the sunset

Did you know that sunsets can be good for your health? Taking a moment to enjoy the last few moments of sun will give you some precious vitamin D to promote the health of your bones, as well as literally taking a step away from the stresses of your day. Pausing to watch the sun go down in the evening will help you appreciate the natural world and bring you directly into the present moment. You could even multitask and take in the sunset whilst running, cycling or enjoying an after-dinner stroll.

Whatever you do, put down your phone and engage in the now. Really look and see how beautiful life is and how inspiring the simple and free things can be. Sunsets are a symbol of renewal and the ongoing passing of time – focusing on it will help you appreciate the natural beauty and power of the Earth. It puts everything else into perspective and ends your day on a calm and reflective note.

LIVE LIFE AS IF
EVERYTHING IS RIGGED
IN YOUR FAVOUR.

RUMI

Make a phone call

Remember when we used to call a friend and chat just for the heck of it? The next time you feel like texting, call instead. Phone calls provide a personal touch that texts often lack. Take a few minutes to catch up with somebody you haven't spoken to in a while and not only will you deepen connections with them, but you'll feel more content too. Aim for at least one meaningful conversation with a different loved one each week.

CLEANSE YOUR SKIN THOROUGHLY

The end of the day is a particularly important time to pay attention to your skin as it will have collected dirt and pollution from the day. You might not have time to do a full face mask, but try to take 5 minutes to indulge in a thorough cleanse, really massaging your skin. Sticking to a daily skincare routine not only benefits the largest organ of your body, it also acts as a form of self-care, promoting relaxation and leaving you with a peaceful mindset.

There are no regrets
in life, just lessons.

Jennifer Aniston

Spill your thoughts with automatic writing

Automatic writing is a type of structured journaling to help you get clear on an issue that's been bugging you. The idea is to write in a free-flowing way, and in doing so cut through all the thoughts that are swirling around in your conscious mind to get to whatever's lurking in your subconscious mind below. It's best done via pen and paper, though you can do it with a keyboard too if you're a fast typist.

Write a question at the top of the page. It can be anything you're currently unsure about. Then set your timer for 5 minutes and start to write your answer. Write fast. Don't stop to edit. Don't take your pen off the page until the time is up. No one is going to see what you've written but you, so it doesn't need to make sense or have perfect spelling and grammar. It's simply a method of getting your thoughts out into the open and becoming clearer on what you need to do next.

ENJOY AN END-OF-THE-DAY STRETCH

Stretching just before you go to bed helps to relax your muscles, as you unwind both physically and mentally and increase flexibility. Whilst your morning stretches may be dynamic and involve movement, evening stretches are often more static. You can stretch the same muscles you moved in the morning, but this time hold the stretch for up to 30 seconds. Aim for evening stretches up to four or five times a week, as your muscles will respond better to this than they would to one longer session.

Read a poem

Poetry will help you pause and connect with your emotions. Read slowly. Every word matters. Reflect on the thoughts that the poem has ignited in your mind and let the words take you out of reality for just a few minutes. You don't have to come up with a complex analysis – there's no correct answer to be found – simply savour it like a good wine. Enjoy the words and allow yourself to connect with the experiences of the poet.

DIFFERENT ROADS SOMETIMES LEAD TO THE SAME CASTLE.

GEORGE R. R. MARTIN

Drink a cup of chamomile tea

Chamomile has some remarkable benefits and has been proven to promote calmness, soothe the stomach and relieve insomnia. Studies have shown that people who drink chamomile tea in the evening have better sleep quality than those who don't. Make a cup of this magic stuff a special part of your evening routine and enjoy it as you reflect on your day. You could even assign a specific mug to the ritual, so your brain will come to associate it with winding down for bedtime.

Envision the miracle

The miracle question is a popular technique used to imagine what life would look like without the current issues and problems that might be holding you back. Take a few moments now to think about the thing that's dragging you down the most – it could be a job you hate, a bad relationship or an unhelpful habit – now close your eyes and imagine yourself free of it.

Then ask yourself, if I woke up tomorrow and I didn't have that job or relationship or habit, how would I know? What would my life look like? What would I look like? What would be happening that's not happening now? If you can envision this future life, then you are one step closer to making it happen, since we can't create what we haven't thought of first. Thinking about what it would be like if it exists is your first step in making it real.

FORGIVE YOURSELF

The relationship you have with yourself is the most important relationship you will ever have. You are worth forgiving. Before you go to sleep tonight, decide what is the one thing you will forgive yourself for. What are you going to let go of? What do you not want to carry with you tomorrow?

You don't have to wait to be confident. Just do it and eventually the confidence will follow.

Carrie Fisher

GIVE YOURSELF A 5-MINUTE FOOT MASSAGE

A foot massage is such a simple thing but is so relaxing. Your feet have carried you all day and now it's time to show them some appreciation. In the process you'll help blood circulation and ease tension, which in turn will help you get a better night's sleep. You don't need fancy oils; any bottle of lotion that you happen to have to hand will do. Rest one foot on the opposite knee and press both thumbs in circular motions across the ball, arch and heel area. Don't forget your ankles and the space between your toes.

Chapter Four

---

*5 Minutes to Start
Something Amazing…*

When we plant seeds in life, we never know which will flourish and which will fail to take root. So we must keep planting. We must keep moving forward. This chapter looks at the things which are easy to start and may grow into a lifelong love. They will take no longer than 5 minutes to begin but could expand into a bigger part of your life if you want them to. Take hold of your life in an active way rather than drifting through it as a passenger who only ever admires the view.

Give back by becoming a volunteer

Take 5 minutes to scout out volunteering opportunities that interest you. There will probably be an online hub showing requests in your area, or if you already have a charity you support, is there more you could do? Think about what you'd like to get out of volunteering. Are you interested in a solo project, a one-off or something more ongoing? Do you want to learn new skills, work with other people and maybe make friends along the way? The right project will be glad of your help.

Write a letter to yourself

It's time to write a letter to a very important person – you. This is not just any letter – this is all about the good things you're doing and how well you're coping with your current challenges. This is a letter of love and appreciation; the kind of letter you would be honoured to receive. What are you proud of? What's gone well recently? What did you cope with? Where did you contribute to your world or your family in a positive way?

By writing this letter you're challenging the critical voice in your head and giving it some positive fuel to work with instead. You're taking stock and focusing on the things that have gone well rather than beating yourself up over the things that didn't work out. Think of yourself as your own best friend who needs some kindness and appreciation as you write it, then put it away to read in the future when you need a boost.

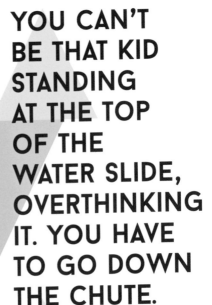

YOU CAN'T
BE THAT KID
STANDING
AT THE TOP
OF THE
WATER SLIDE,
OVERTHINKING
IT. YOU HAVE
TO GO DOWN
THE CHUTE.

Tina Fey

Relight your fire with a new hobby

Is there a hobby you used to love but haven't picked up in ages? Or something that you always meant to try but never quite got round to? Research a new hobby or craft project – even better if it's something you can do with your hands that isn't scrolling through your phone. If you're feeling nervous about it, call a friend and ask them if they'd like to join you. Gather or order any equipment you might need and make an appointment in your diary for when you're going to do it.

SEW ON A BUTTON

Taking a few minutes for repairs will help your favourite clothes last longer, and by re-wearing instead of buying new you'll be helping the planet too! What's that minor repair you've been meaning to make to your most-loved item of clothing? If you're not sure how to approach this, there are plenty of YouTube tutorial videos that might be able to help.

IMPERFECTIONS ARE NOT INADEQUACIES; THEY ARE REMINDERS THAT WE'RE ALL IN THIS TOGETHER.

BRENÉ BROWN

Pay it forward

Think about the last time someone did something nice for you. What put an unexpected smile on your face? Now, what could you do to pass that smile on? You could: pay for someone else's coffee; tip a little bit more than usual; donate unworn clothes to a charity; do a friend's household chore without being asked; bring in baked goods for your team at work; give the next person who impresses you a genuine compliment; spend time getting to know someone even if you don't think they're your cup of tea.

These actions of paying it forward to someone new bring double benefits because they make both you and others feel good. Improving your relationships in this way creates emotional warmth, releasing the feel-good hormone oxytocin (also known as the love hormone). And by focusing on appreciating the kindness done to you and using it to fuel something new, you will feel more connected and part of a community. It's the ultimate win–win scenario.

Challenge your brain

What kind of puzzles do you enjoy? Maybe a sudoku, jigsaw, crossword or quiz? What method of stimulating the brain would be fun for you? Do that for 5 minutes. Solving puzzles improves your mental speed and can be particularly good for improving short-term memory. By doing a puzzle you're exercising both sides of your brain – the logical and creative sides. Focusing on a puzzle is also great for stress levels, since it forces you to concentrate on one thing only, and step away from any other worries you might have.

NOT EVERYTHING THAT IS FACED CAN BE CHANGED, BUT NOTHING CAN BE CHANGED UNTIL IT IS FACED.

JAMES BALDWIN

EXPAND A CONVERSATION BEYOND HELLO

It's the minor interactions we have with other people that deepen our relationships in the long run. If you find it a struggle to talk to new people, challenge yourself today to take at least one interaction beyond "hello". Perhaps a simple but sincere enquiry about someone's day or a compliment on their outfit could lead to a more meaningful relationship, whether in person or through an online meeting. Ask questions and really listen to the answers. It doesn't have to be a big conversation, remember that these are just 5-minute tasks.

TAKE THE FIRST STEP ON YOUR PATH TO HAPPINESS

Write down three things that make you happy. Is there something you've never tried that you've always thought might make you happy? Plan to do at least one of them by the end of the week. If there's an everyday thing that brings you joy, aim to do it as often as you can. Everyone has space for more happiness in their life.

Security is not having things:
it's handling things.

Susan Jeffers

SQUEEZE IN A SIDE HUSTLE

Do you have something that you do on the side that you'd really like to become your main job? What would you need to do to make that happen? What do you need to learn? Who do you need to connect with? Make a list of the things your side hustle will need in order to grow and try to tick one thing off a day.

Identify what is draining you

This is a tip for anyone who feels frustrated with how much they're getting done each day. Often the reason people don't achieve as much as they'd like to is because of a lack of energy rather than a lack of time. One easy way to gain more energy is to identify and eliminate anything that's draining your energy in the first place. You don't have to do this all at once, but start to make a plan to shift the energy suckers in your life.

Write down ten things that are draining you right now. Where in your day does your energy start to sag? Anything could be affecting it, such as a late bedtime, being surrounded by clutter, or a relationship that isn't working anymore. Divide up your list into the things you can control and the things you can't. Focus your efforts on the things you can change — eliminating them will make the biggest difference. Look for the easiest change you could make and start there.

Nourish your cultural side

A healthy diet is important, but don't forget that your mind needs nourishing too. Treat your brain to a cultural snack! Read the first few pages of a book that interests you, check out what's on Netflix and plan your next watch, or book a ticket to an exhibition or play – there are plenty of online options you could make the most of, like virtual gallery tours. What have you always meant to do but never quite got around to?

PIONEERING IS
NEVER DONE
IN FRONT OF
CHEERLEADERS
URGING ON
A ROARING
GRANDSTAND
OF POPULAR
APPROVAL.

George Takei

Answer your calling

When something is a calling in life, it doesn't usually go away – instead it tends to get louder. What calling have you been ignoring, even though the whispering in your ear may have turned to shouting? What do you know in your heart that you really need to do? Is there something that's interested you for a long time but you've never acted on the urge? Take the first step in making it a reality by writing down your calling and outlining what you need to do to get there or researching it online.

Clear out a corner

A full declutter might be too much to take on, so why not start with a corner, a drawer, a table or a chair? Choose a small space and remove everything from it. Just sweep it all away. Clean the clear surface and only put back what you want to be there. The rest can either go wherever it's meant to live in the house, be donated to a charity shop or repurposed.

TRY SOMETHING NEW

Challenge your assumption of who you are. Wear different colour clothing that's out of your comfort zone. Order something for lunch that you've never tried before. Wear your hair a different way. Strike up a conversation with someone you see every day but have never spoken to. We often let the fear of the unknown stop us from embracing new things, but shaking up your daily habits stimulates creativity and provokes a whole host of thoughts you might never have had.

YOU ARE RESPONSIBLE
FOR YOUR LIFE AND
WHEN YOU GET THAT,
EVERYTHING CHANGES.

OPRAH WINFREY

Identify your long-term goals

It's time to take a wider view on where your life is going, and how that differs from where you want it to go. Picture yourself ten years from now. What would you like to have done in your life by then? Write down five things and be as ambitious and creative as you like – it's a decade away, and anything can happen by then, right? Where would you like to go? What job would you like to be doing? Where would you be living? Who would you be spending time with?

Then shuffle back a little closer in time. How about five years from now? What progress should you have made towards your ultimate goals by then? If you were halfway there, what would that look like? Shuffle a little closer again – what about in one year's time? Or six months? How much progress might you have made? Trace the timeline back until you see what small action you can take today and tomorrow to help you reach that long-term goal.

SOMETIMES WHEN YOU'RE IN A DARK PLACE YOU THINK YOU'VE BEEN BURIED, BUT YOU'VE ACTUALLY BEEN PLANTED.

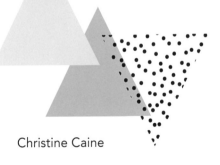

Christine Caine

THAT IS THE KEY TO NAVIGATING THIS LIFE — DON'T TAKE IT TOO SERIOUSLY. THAT'S WHEN THE PARTY BEGINS.

RUPAUL

Conclusion

Now that you've got some ideas for things you *could* do, it's time to pin yourself down to the things you *will* do. Which of the tips you've read so far have stuck with you? When did you feel most inspired? Pick your favourite one or two and decide when you will start. Make a commitment to yourself to try it for a week or two and see how you get on.

While some of these tips are one-offs, others have the potential to become a new daily habit and could transform the way you live your life. All of life is a work in progress, so feel free to tweak or change anything that's not working for you to make it fit you better. Start with something easy so you really feel how simple it can be to change your life. Track what you're doing in a journal and come back to it in a month so you can see what progress you've made. You have the power to choose your new direction, and the world will open up to you when you do. In years to come you will thank yourself for everything you do now. So take that step. You've got this! See you on the other side.

If you're interested in finding out
more about our books, find us on Facebook at
Summersdale Publishers and follow us
on Twitter at **@Summersdale**.

www.summersdale.com

IMAGE CREDITS

pp.1, 4, 5, 7, 8, 12, 19, 25, 32, 33, 36, 38, 39, 46, 49, 53, 59,
64, 65, 68, 69, 75, 79, 86, 87, 91, 94, 97, 98, 103, 106, 107,
111, 118, 126, 127 © marmarto/Shutterstock.com